Another Point of View

HELP YOURSELF, LITTLE RED HEN!

by Dr. Alvin Granowsky

illustrations by Jane Manning

STECK-VAUGHN
COMPANY
ELEMENTARY • SECONDARY • ADULT • LIBRARY

Papa Pig always told us little piglets, "You must learn to take care of yourself. Carry your own weight, and you'll do well. That's the only way to get out of the mudhole and make a place for yourself in life."

My papa's words have helped me all my life. That's why I was so upset about the little red hen.

The little red hen never did a thing for herself. She would always ask Miss Cat, Mr. Duck, or me to do her work for her.

"Mr. Duck," she would ask, "Would you mind picking up that hoe and helping me chop down a few little weeds?"

4

"Miss Cat, how would you like to help me rake some leaves this morning?" she might ask.

"Mr. Pig, I know you would love to help me sweep my front porch," she would say in her sweetest little hen voice.

5

We were happy to help her. But one day, we noticed that we weren't just helping her. We were doing all the work!

It was Miss Cat who first said out loud what we were all thinking. "How will the little red hen ever learn to do anything for herself if we always do it for her?" she asked.

Mr. Duck and I agreed. So right then and there, the three of us decided to help the little red hen. We would teach her to do things for herself.

We didn't have to wait long to begin our plan. The very next day, the little red hen found a lovely grain of wheat. "Who will help me plant this wheat?" she asked.

Mr. Duck, Miss Cat, and I answered, "You must plant it yourself." It was hard for us to be so tough with her. But, we knew it was best for the little red hen.

"Well then, I will!" said the little red hen. You could tell she was angry by the way she threw the wheat to the ground. "Grow!" she said and stomped away.

Well, the wheat would not grow just lying there on the ground. So, Mr. Duck, Miss Cat, and I planted and watered the wheat while the little red hen wasn't looking.

11

Soon, the wheat grew tall. It needed to be cut. "Who will help me cut the wheat?" asked the little red hen.

Well, she could only learn by doing it. So, Mr. Duck, Miss Cat, and I said, "You must cut the wheat by yourself."

"Well then, I will!" said the little red hen. She was so angry that she gave the stalk a big **wHACK!** and it came tumbling down.

"There you go!" we cheered. "We knew you could do it."

13

"I can do whatever I set my mind to!" said the little red hen. She seemed so proud of herself, and a little surprised, too. Our plan was starting to work.

Then the little red hen asked, "Who will help me thresh my wheat? I hope I don't have to do that all by myself as well."

Mr. Duck, Miss Cat, and I just smiled. The little red hen was beginning to learn. "Yes," we all said. "Since that is your wheat, you must thresh it all by yourself."

So the little red hen threshed the wheat all by herself. When she was done, she was very proud.

Then the little red hen said, "It is time to take the grain to the mill. Who will help me?"

"You can do it," I said.

16

So Mr. Duck, Miss Cat, and I watched
proudly as the little red hen set off for the mill.
We could see that we were helping her. She
was learning to do things for herself.

Soon the little red hen came back from the mill with a sack of fine flour. She was very proud. "Now I am going to use this flour to make some dough. Who will help me?" she asked.

"Don't you want to try it on your own?" we asked. "You've done it all by yourself so far."

Then the little red hen cried, "I don't know how to turn flour into dough! No one ever showed me how!" Great big tears rolled from her little hen eyes.

19

"We will tell you how to do it," said Mr. Duck.

"But we will not do it for you," said Miss Cat.

"You will have to do it for yourself after we tell you how," I said.

So we explained to the little red hen the
way to turn flour into dough. And do you know
what? The little red hen did a fine job. She
was so proud of herself.

21

Then the little red hen popped the dough into the oven. As it baked, the bread smelled delicious.

You should have seen the pride on the little red hen's face as she took the bread from the oven. "Doesn't this bread look wonderful?" she asked. "Now who would like to help me eat it?"

"Why, we will help you eat it!" said Mr. Duck, Miss Cat, and I. We were so proud of that little hen.

But the little red hen had another idea. "I did all the work myself. So now I will eat the bread myself!" And that is exactly what she did!

Mr. Duck, Miss Cat, and I were happy. We helped the little red hen learn a lesson about doing things for herself. But we all agree that our work with her is not done yet. We still need to teach the little red hen to share!

Another Point of View

The Little Red Hen

retold by Dr. Alvin Granowsky
illustrations by Wendy Edelson

STECK-VAUGHN
C O M P A N Y
ELEMENTARY • SECONDARY • ADULT • LIBRARY

Once upon a time, the little red hen
found a grain of wheat in the barnyard. "What
a lovely grain of wheat," said the little red hen.
"I think I will plant it."

"Who will help me plant this wheat?"
the little red hen asked the other animals
in the barnyard.

"Not I," said the duck.

"Not I," said the cat.

"Not I," said the pig.

"Then I will do it myself!" said the little red hen. And that is exactly what she did.

Each day the little red hen watered the wheat and pulled the weeds around it. After a while, the wheat grew into a tall stalk.

When the wheat was ripe, the little red
hen asked, "Who will help me cut the wheat?"

"Not I," said the duck.

"Not I," said the cat.

"Not I," said the pig.

"Then I will do it myself!" said the little red hen. And that is exactly what she did.

After the wheat was cut, it needed to be threshed. "Who will help me thresh the wheat?" asked the little red hen.

"Not I," said the duck.

"Not I," said the cat.

"Not I," said the pig.

"Then I will do it myself!" said the little red hen. And that is exactly what she did.

Soon the little red hen had a sack of grain.
"Who will help me take the grain to the mill?"
asked the little red hen.

"Not I," said the duck.

"Not I," said the cat.

"Not I," said the pig.

"Then I will do it myself!" said the little red hen. And that is exactly what she did.

The mill ground the wheat into a fine flour just right for making bread. The little red hen carried the sack of flour home.

15

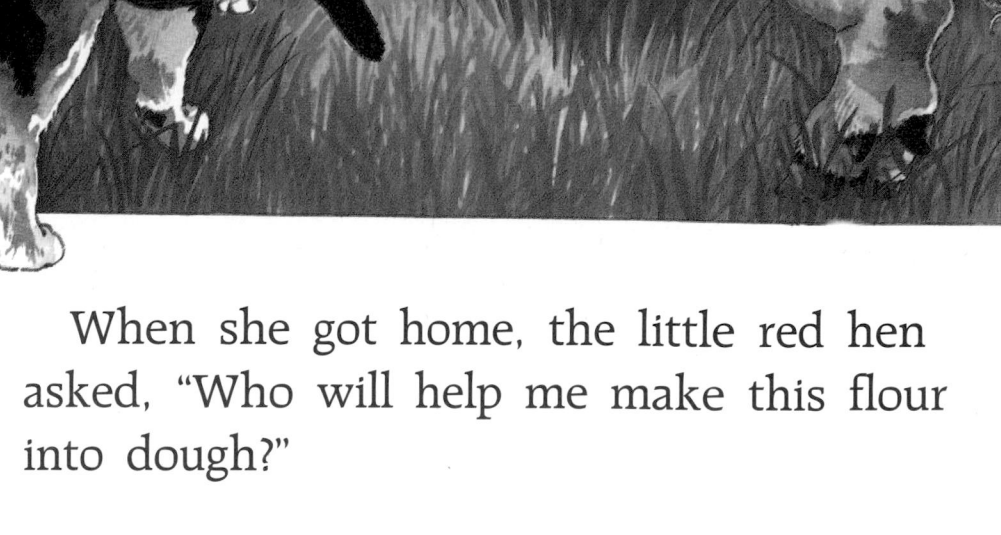

When she got home, the little red hen
asked, "Who will help me make this flour
into dough?"

"Not I," said the duck.

"Not I," said the cat.

"Not I," said the pig.

"Then I will do it myself!" said the little
red hen. And that is exactly what she did.

When the dough was ready, the little red hen put it into the oven to bake. Soon, a **delicious** smell filled the air.

When the bread was baked, the little red hen took it out of the oven.

"Now, who will help me eat the bread?"
asked the little red hen.

"I will!" said the duck.

"I will!" said the cat.

"I will!" said the pig.

But the little red hen said, "Oh, no.
All by myself, I
   planted the wheat,
   cut the wheat,
   threshed the wheat,
   took the grain to the mill,
   made the flour into dough,
   and baked the dough into bread.

So now, all by myself, I am going to eat
the bread."

And that is exactly what she did!